A SOW CALLED SODA

STORY BY WENDY WHARAM

PICTURES BY
IVAN RIPLEY

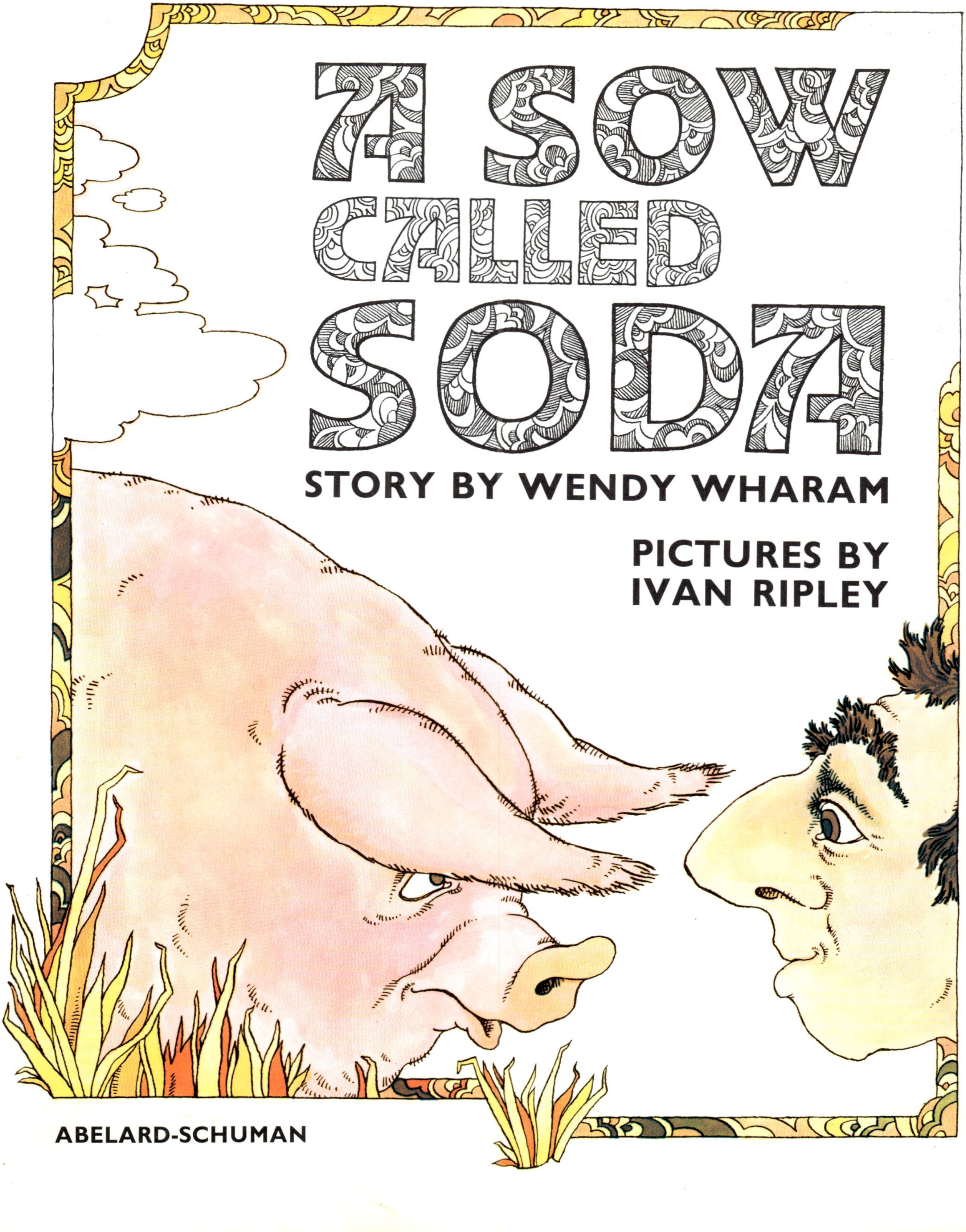

ABELARD-SCHUMAN

First Published Abelard-Schuman Limited 1974
ISBN: 0 200 72116 X (Hardback)
0 200 72117 8 (Paperback)

Printed in Great Britain

Soda was a sow.
She was as big as a cow,
and twice as strong.
She was fat and pink—and fierce.

Mr. Pooter owned Soda.
Or did Soda own Mr. Pooter?
Mr. Pooter was a tiny man
and Soda was so big,
that it was easy to see
who was boss.
Not tiny Mr. Pooter,
who wouldn't dare to
say "Boo" to a goose.

**If he said "Boo" to Soda,
she'd tip him in the pig trough,
which she did—often.**

Through the middle of Soda's field
ran the path to the village.
The children used it on their way to school.
So did Miss Brass, the teacher, Mr. Biggs, the postman,
and Mr. Brown, the butcher.

**Soda didn't like them to come through her field.
When she saw the children coming down the path,
she chased them
and knocked them down in the mud.**

When she saw Miss Brass,
the teacher,
coming down the path,
Soda charged at her.

Miss Brass hit Soda
with her umbrella.
Soda tipped her neatly
into the pig trough.

Miss Brass's new hat floated sadly
on top of the water.
Soda fished it out, and put it on.
She looked at herself in the water.
"What a charming pig I am," said Soda.

Mr. Pooter
fished out Miss Brass,
who was very cross.
She tried to hit him
with her umbrella.
"That pig," she said,
"is not safe,
She should be
under lock and key."

But Mr. Pooter
had just seen Soda
in Miss Brass's new hat.
"Well, fancy that.
A pig in a hat."
Miss Brass didn't think
that was at all funny.
"You must buy me
a new hat, Mr. Pooter,"
she said angrily.

Next down the path came Mr. Biggs, the postman, on his red bicycle.

Soda chased him.
Mr. Biggs fell off his bicycle,
and all his letters fell out of the sack.
Before he could stop her,
Soda ate six letters and a parcel.

Mr. Biggs shouted, "You'll pay for this, Mr. Pooter."
Mr. Pooter said sadly,
"Soda's a big pig.
Big pigs get very hungry."

Seven people were very angry
in the village that day.
"Where are our letters?"
they shouted at Mr. Biggs.
"Soda has eaten them," said Mr. Biggs.

Next, down the path came Bill,
the butcher's boy.
He had a basket
of pork sausages over his arm.
Soda couldn't bear sausages.
A cousin of hers
had been made
into sausage meat
only the week before.

Soda chased Bill, the butcher's boy,
but Bill was too quick for her.

He shinned up a tree,
and pelted sausages
at Soda.

Soda pushed at the tree with her snout so hard
that she managed to uproot it.
The tree crashed to the ground and
so did Bill, the butcher's boy.
He was so sore that he had to stay in bed for a week.

One day, a large crowd of people came to see Mr. Pooter. There were the schoolchildren, Miss Brass, Mr. Biggs, Bill, the butcher's boy, Mr. Brown, the butcher, and Mr. Donkin.

Mr. Donkin was the Mayor,
a very important man.
He showed Mr. Pooter a letter, with all the people's names. "We've all agreed, Soda must go,"
said Mr. Donkin.

"But I'm fond of Soda," said Mr. Pooter.
"She doesn't mean to be bad."
Mr. Brown, the butcher, stepped forward.
"That sow's not safe. I'll buy her from you.
She'll make fine sausage meat."
Mr. Donkin said, "We'll give you a week
to think it over."

Mr. Pooter went to see Soda.
"I'll not let them make you into sausage meat, old girl."
At the word sausage meat,
Soda went wild.
She tipped Mr. Pooter into the pig trough again.
"Good girl," spluttered Mr. Pooter,
as he came up for air,
"You won't let anyone push you around."

In the field next to Soda's some houses were going up.
The men were busy clearing the site.
They had a bulldozer at work,
to uproot the trees.
One day, the bulldozer broke down.
They couldn't get it to go at all.
The men said, "We're fed up. It's always breaking down.
We'll never get the site cleared."

Soda pushed through the hedge,
and ran at the tree with all her strength.
It toppled and fell.
The men were so amazed,
they just stood and stared,
as Soda felled tree after tree.

The men sent for Mr. Pooter.
"We'd like to give Soda a job," the boss said.
"Just look at that."
So Mr. Pooter watched, as Soda uprooted the trees.

He sent for Mr. Donkin, the mayor, and Mr. Brown, the butcher. "Look at that," he said. "There's a pig for you."

No one mentioned again
about making sausage meat out of Soda.
She was far too busy felling trees,
to charge at Miss Brass, the teacher,
or Bill, the butcher's boy,
or Mr. Biggs, the postman.

She was even too tired, at the end of a hard day, to tip Mr. Pooter into the pig trough. This made Mr. Pooter a little sad. “Soda,” he said, “isn’t the same sow at all.”